# DESERT AIRFORCE

# DESERT AIRFORCE

DAVIS MONTHAN A.F.B. ARIZONA
**Philip Chinnery**

**Airlife**
England

# Acknowledgements

The author would like to thank the following people for their assistance with the preparation of this book:

Captain Mark Besich, PAO HQ 836 Air Division
Technical Sergeant Marc Brazil, AMARC Tour Guide
Ms Sally Ann McCulley
Ms Donna L Clark, Historian
Ms Terry Minch, AMARC/XPX
Mr Bob Greby, Photographer
Ms Mary Gentry, Pima Air Museum
Mr Bob Hoover
Mr Richard Calder, USIS London
Mr Bob Shane, Photographer
Mr Graham Robson, Photographer
Owen and Kate Mendota

and all the personnel at AMARC who willingly gave up their time to help me with my research. I hope they will be pleased with the final product.

All pictures taken by Philip Chinnery and Sally McCulley unless otherwise credited.

Copyright © Philip Chinnery 1989

First published 1989
by Airlife Publishing Ltd.

British Library Cataloguing in Publication Data
Chinnery, Philip
    Desert airforce
    1. American military forces. Disused
    military aircraft
    1. Title
    623.74'6'0973

ISBN 1 85310 073 0 Case Bound
ISBN 1 85310 074 9 Paperback

## Airlife Publishing Ltd.

7 St. John's Hill, Shrewsbury, England.

# Introduction

As any resident of Tucson, Arizona, will confirm, you can see all sorts of things in the desert. One of the more interesting sights to behold in the Sonora Desert just outside Tucson is visible from the port windows of the airliners on approach to Tucson International Airport. Rows and rows of aircraft tails can be identified in the distance as the Desert Boneyard or, more accurately, the Aerospace Maintenance and Regeneration Centre, comes into view.

AMARC is not a mirage, as anyone driving down the Golf Links Road past the perimeter fence will appreciate. The centre is vast and has been there for more than forty years. Its origins in fact can be traced back to the final days of the Second World War.

The war came to an abrupt end with the exploding of atomic bombs over Hiroshima and Nagasaki in the autumn of 1945, and shortly thereafter America's fleets of war-weary aircraft began to return home. Airfields throughout the south-western United States began to echo with the sound of bombers and fighters arriving back after years of war. They were parked in rows and left to await their fate.

Most of the fighters and bombers were fast becoming obselete, and there were simply too many non-combat types for the peacetime needs of the United States. Within a matter of months the Government had decided to dispose of the 65,000 aircraft, a decision which no doubt caused the aircraft manufacturers to breathe a heavy sigh of relief. The War Assets Administration was tasked with the job of arranging the disposal of the vast numbers of aircraft. The 35,000 non-combat aircraft such as trainers and transports could be sold on the open market to the public, but for the 30,000 combat aircraft there could be only one fate.

Within months, smelters were operating at places such as Kingman Army Air Field in Arizona, where over 5,000 aircraft were drained of fuel and scrapped. However, despite the almost indecent haste in which thousands of Liberators, Flying Fortresses, Havocs and the like were being fed into the smelters, an iron curtain was descending across Europe and it was decided that at least some aircraft should be kept and stored as insurance against a future outbreak of hostilities.

The decision to be made now was where to store this reserve of aircraft. Several possible sites were visited and Davis-Monthan Field, to the south east of Tucson, Arizona, was chosen as a permanent storage area. The field was formerly the city's municipal airport and was named after two Air Service Officers from Tucson, who were killed in separate aviation accidents in the early 1920s: Lieutenants Samuel H Davis and Oscar Monthan.

The main reasons for the choice were the low annual rainfall (eleven inches per year), low humidity (ten to twenty per cent), and the fact that the soil in that part of the Sonora Desert, known as 'Caliche', has a low acidic content which is ideal for long-term storage, and is baked so hard that aircraft can be parked on it without needing tarmac or concrete stands.

The 4105th Army Air Force Base Unit (Air Base) was established at Davis-Monthan on 15 November 1945, and under the direction of HQ San Antonio Air Technical Service Command the first surplus B-29 and C-47 aircraft began to arrive for storage. The task of the 4105th in the early days was simply the processing and preservation from corrosion of all aircraft selected for storage, and by 31 July 1946, 650 B-29s, 250 C-47s and eighteen museum aircraft were in storage.

In 1947 the Fort Pitt Packaging Company was awarded a contract to 'cocoon' 486 of the 679 B-29s then in storage, under guidelines provided by the 8th Air Force. The process involved the application by spraying of four layers of plastic to form a tough rawhide-like covering which should last up to ten years. Bags of dessicant (silica gel) were placed inside the fuselage and engine nacelles to absorb any excess moisture which may have been trapped.

The 4105th was renamed the 3040th Aircraft Storage Depot in August 1948, and reclamation and salvage was added to its mission. Forty-seven B-29s and fourteen of the museum aircraft were earmarked for reclamation, and by the end of 1948 the inventory had dropped to 535 B-29s and 187 C-47s. This reduction was mainly due to the expansion of Strategic Air Command and the Berlin Airlift which had depleted the Air Force's transportation assets.

Almost two-thirds of the B-29s returned to service in 1950. The Royal Air Force received the first eighty-seven in March, and within two weeks of the outbreak of the Korean War in June Headquarters Air Material Command ordered the removal from storage of fifty more for overhaul and reconditioning by the Grand Central Aircraft Company at Tucson Airport.

With the introduction of the B-47 bomber in 1951, and the end of the Korean War in 1953, SAC began to retire its B-29 fleet. By the end of 1953 the number of B-29s in storage had doubled to 340 and other types had begun to arrive, including twenty-nine Grumman SA-16 amphibians, 120 North American T-6 trainers and twenty-one Boeing QB-17 Flying Fortress drones.

In anticipation of the arrival of many more aircraft, the storage area was increased by half to 1,290 acres and the Centre's mission requirement became that of aircraft storage and preservation, spare parts reclamation, and the removal of aircraft from storage and preparation for one-time flight to an overhaul depot.

The numbers of aircraft in storage began to grow rapidly throughout the 1950s. By the end of 1956 almost 1,300 aircraft were in storage, including 350 B-29s and over 600 T-6s. The B-29 salvage programme was in full swing and 120 had already gone into the smelters for melting down into ingots. Other types had begun to arrive, including

B-26s, B-50s, F-80s, F-84s, F-86s and the first fifty of the giant B-36 Peacemakers.

The 3040th was renamed the Arizona Aircraft Storage Branch in June 1956 and then redesignated the 2704th Air Force Aircraft Storage and Disposition Group in August 1959, reporting directly to HQ Air Force Logistics Command. By that time the number of aircraft in storage had more than trebled to over 4,300. Only a handful of B-29s and B-36s now remained. In their place were parked hundreds of B-25s, C-45s, F-86s, T-28s, and at least two dozen other types of aircraft.

The emphasis was now on disposal rather than storage. An Air Force Disposal Division was organized to handle the redistribution and marketing of surplus aircraft, and the operation of the government smelters was turned over to civilian contractors. The mission of the 2704th was consequently expanded in January 1960 to include the redistribution of excess USAF aircraft and the disposal by sale of any obsolete aircraft unwanted by the other services, government or federal agencies, or foreign governments.

It was then decided to consolidate all existing aircraft storage facilities under a single manager inter-service operation. Thus on 1 February 1965 the 2704th was renamed the Military Aircraft Storage and Disposition Centre (MASDC).

The US Army began to store its obsolete H-21 helicopters at MASDC in August 1965, with the Coast Guard following suit in 1967. The Navy moved 900 of its aircraft to Davis-Monthan Air Force Base and closed its Litchfield Park Storage facility on 1 July 1967. The size of the storage area at MASDC had increased to 2,800 acres, and by the end of 1967 4,000 aircraft of forty-six different types were in storage.

Despite the intense reorganization taking place at MASDC, the commander of the Centre, Colonel I R Perkin, was farsighted enough to become the driving force behind a plan to establish a local aviation museum in Tucson. With MASDC on its doorstep, the museum would never be short of exhibits, and over the years the Pima Air Museum has grown into one of the largest in the United States with 100,000 visitors each year.

Rather more colourful than its Air Force neighbour, North American T-39D Sabreliner 150548 served with Navy Training Squadron VT-10 until its retirement in 1985.

At this time the United States was heavily involved in the Vietnam War and the centre's workload increased drastically. The need for counter-insurgency aircraft led to the withdrawal and despatch to overhaul and modification facilities of large numbers of A-1 Skyraiders, B-26 Invaders, C-47 Skytrains and T-28 Trojans.

Combat losses amongst the Navy aircraft carrier squadrons had to be made good by withdrawing mothballed A-4 Skyhawks and F-8 Crusaders, and 160 were flown out in the first few months of 1967. High on the priority list were B-52 engines, and 266 were removed and shipped to South East Asia in the same year.

By 1970 the B-58 Hustler bomber fleet had been received for storage and eventual disposal, and the first early-model B-52s had arrived. The rundown of units in South East Asia caused the MASDC inventory to reach an all-time high of 6,080 aircraft and twenty-one missiles in the summer of 1973. Approximately 2,500 belonged to the Air Force, 1,900 to the Navy and 1,500 to the Army.

One use has been found for many of the fighters rendered obsolete by the introduction of newer types such as the Phantom, F-15 and F-16. The Air Force decided to replace its subscale Firebee target drones with life-size radio-controlled pilotless aircraft, and in 1973 the Sperry Corporation was awarded a contract to convert 215 surplus F-102 Delta Daggers, in storage at MASDC.

Following the success of the F-102s as target drones, Sperry converted eighty of the 400 F-100 Super Sabres at MASDC, and Flight Systems Incorporated commenced the conversion of 209 more. The last thirty-five F-100Fs will be delivered by 1990. Eventually this will be followed by a programme called Pacer Six, involving the conversion of some 200 F-106 Delta Darts currently in storage at AMARC. The first aircraft is scheduled to leave in Spring 1989.

The number of aircraft in storage has been steadily declining since the post-Vietnam days of the seventies, and as the priorities of the armed forces have changed, so the centre has had to move with the times. In 1985, in a determined attempt to change its 'aircraft boneyard' image, MASDC

Navy Douglas TA-4B Skyhawks currently in storage, with 142871 nearest the camera.

was renamed The Aerospace Maintenance and Regeneration Centre (AMARC). The aim of this book is to describe the present day occupants and workload of AMARC. For comparison, readers may like to obtain the book *Desert Boneyard*, by the same author and publisher. In that book, the complete history of the centre and the aircraft that have passed through it since 1945, are shown in the same format as this work.

The processing of aircraft into storage has changed since the early days of the B-29s, but it is no less complex a procedure. On arrival all explosives, such as ejection seat charges, are removed, together with any pilferable or particularly valuable items. The aircraft is then washed to remove industrial or marine residues and inspected for corrosion. Navy aircraft, especially those on aircraft carriers, have usually been exposed to corrosive salt air and require anti-corrosion treatment.

The aircraft is then towed to the Preservation Farm where mechanics drain the engines and hydraulic lines of oil. They also drain the fuel from the aircraft and then pump in a light weight oil, which is again drained, leaving a protective oil film in the lines and tanks to protect them from drying out or corroding.

Engine intakes and exhausts are then covered with paper and any seams, inspection hatches, openings and rubber seals in the upper half of the aircraft are taped. The paper, tape and any fragile surfaces such as canopies and radomes are then sprayed with a heavy, plastic-like material called Spraylat. A black coat is applied first, followed by a white coat to relect sunlight. The underside of the aircraft, the wheel wells, drainage holes and other openings are not treated, and are left open to allow circulation of air and minimize condensation.

Although Spraylat does a good job protecting the aircraft from sand, dust and the elements, its main purpose is to maintain the internal temperature of the aircraft at roughly five degrees above that of the surrounding air. Without such protection, the temperature inside the aircraft could reach 200°F, causing damage to rubber parts and functional components. When the aircraft is

Overleaf: The prototype Boeing 707 N70700 has been stored at AMARC on behalf of the Smithsonian Institute since 1976.
*(Bob Greby)*

required to fly again, the Spraylat can be peeled off easily and the preservation process reversed.

With the high cost of purchasing new aircraft, the number of aircraft being scrapped has declined since the 1960s and 1970s, and many uses are found for the obsolete aircraft stored at AMARC. Many return to service with the Air Force, Navy, Marines, Army or Coast Guard, and inter-service transfers are not uncommon. Foreign military sales are also a good source of revenue, and in recent years these have included obsolete Navy S-2 Trackers sold to Peru and F-4 Phantoms to the British Royal Air Force.

Overleaf: Having been in storage since 1972, Douglas KA-3B Skywarrior 138969 has suffered extensive spare parts reclamation.

Opposite: A good zoom lens brings the Sonora Mountains closer to this Grumman EA-6A Prowler parked near the wash rack.

Below: Fifteen years of desert sun have failed to fade the markings of this Douglas EKA-3B Skywarrior, which once served with Navy Tactical Electronic Warfare Squadron VAQ-135.

Many state and local government agencies benefited from the disposal of the Army's surplus helicopters in the post-Vietnam years. The Customs Service utilizes ex-Army OV-1 Mohawks for border patrol, and the California Division of Forestry has been given a large number of S-2 Trackers for conversion to fire bombers.

Any tax-supported organization may request the donation of obsolete aircraft from AMARC, including schools, museums and veteran organizations. In the last couple of years, the Air Force Heritage programme has resulted in the migration of dozens of aircraft to new homes at air base museums or on the gates of air bases. One major recent project begun by AMARC involves Battle Damage Repair Training courses, carried out in a secluded part of the storage area where aircraft are 'shot up' and repaired. The importance attached to this BDRT training has led to the shipment of many surplus F-4 and F-101 fighters to air bases in the States, and particularly in Europe.

Approximately half of the aircraft sent to AMARC for storage will fly again, and of the

remainder, half will be used as a source of spare parts for aircraft still in service. When these aircraft have been picked clean, they will be earmarked for disposal by the local office of the Defense Reutilization and Marketing Service and sold. Sales catalogues are sent to eligible bidders who are allowed to inspect the aircraft; they are then invited to submit sealed bids for the aircraft in their current 'as is' state. Recent sales have included Boeing 707 airliners, following their reclamation for parts for Air Force KC-135s, largely intact Navy P-2 Neptune patrol aircraft and KA-3B Skywarrior carcasses.

Generally, most aircraft offered for sale find their way into one of the handful of scrap and storage yards bordering the perimeter of AMARC. The largest of these is AMCEP, which is owned by Bob Hoover, who informed the author that he had purchased the Boeing 707s and P-2 Neptunes. The former were being scrapped, together with most of the P-2s, but some have been kept for sale to warbird enthusiasts. The smelting of aircraft still goes on in the local yards and it can be a profitable business; some aircraft such as the A-4 Skyhawk are much sought after due to the precious metals and alloys that can be reclaimed.

Below: With its nose supported by wooden props, Douglas KA-3B Skywarrior 138906 was retired by Navy Tactical Electronic Warfare Squadron VAQ-208 in September 1971.

Opposite: Over 120 Navy Vought Corsair IIs are in storage. A-7E 156807 nearest the camera used to serve on the USS Saratoga.

The centre that supplies the local yards with their work kindly gave the author full access to all areas and departments, and more than convinced him that they are living up to their new high-tech Maintenance and Regeneration Centre image. The efficiency of the centre cannot be doubted, and the enthusiasm of the employees operating the real time X-ray machine, when showing the author the crack discovered in an F-100 tail assembly, was sincere. The workings of the centre are, to say the least, impressive.

The major programmes currently underway are as follows:

Contingency aircraft maintenance
F-100 Drone programme
F-106 Drone programme
KC-135 aircraft support programme
Specialized Repair Activity Workloads
Aircraft Battle Damage Repair
Titan Missile Storage
Reclamation
Weapon System Phase-out Management

In addition, AMARC now stores production tooling for aircraft types that are no longer in production, such as the A-10 ground attack aircraft and the B-1 bomber. Should the need arise to remanufacture any component, the tooling can be located and shipped to a contractor. The tooling is coated with a product called Pro Cote 129, which is similar in appearance to clear varnish and should preserve the tooling for five to seven years.

The centre is also being utilized for the destruction of missiles as a part of the Intermediate-Range Nuclear Forces Treaty verification process. Under the INF treaty, 429 Air Force Cruise missiles and more than 100 Army Pershing 2 missiles are to be destroyed. The missile warheads are removed before the missiles arrive at AMARC and the fuel, worth fourteen dollars a gallon, is also removed and reused. The guidance set and jet engine are also saved and can be reused in the Navy's Tomahawk sea-launched cruise missiles. The missiles and their transporter-erector launchers are then destroyed by cutting the weapons in half lengthwise, while a Soviet vertification team watches the process.

Item number 15 in sale number 41-6304, this Douglas C-118 Liftmaster awaits the smelter in the Southwestern Alloys scrapyard just across the road from AMARC.

The contingency aircraft withdrawal programme brings to mind the B-29 bomber war reserve of the late 1940s. Both the Navy and Air Force require certain types of aircraft to be available for rapid return to service. In an attempt to facilitate the quick withdrawal from storage and return to service of these aircraft, both services have been carrying out bagging projects to replace the Spray-latting of the aircraft. The Navy placed the new covers on twenty-four F-4s, and the Air Force used twenty-two covers on seven different types of aircraft and helicopter. This method would have been faster and cheaper than the conventional Spraylatting procedure, but the latest report suggests that the tests have proven unsatisfactory, and the use of the covers may be discontinued. Confirmation is awaited, but in the meantime aviation photographers may breathe a sigh of relief.

As this book went to press, the wheels have been set in motion at AMARC to receive approximately 6,000 Army aircraft over the next twenty years, as the Army carries out its aviation modernization plan. Some 2,300 of the Army's 3,400 UH-1 Hueys will be retired in favour of the newer, larger, more powerful UH-60 Blackhawk. The first of the UH-1s have already arrived at AMARC, together with some OH-58 Kiowa helicopters. Other types to follow include the OH-6A Cayuse, CH-54 Tarhe, AH-1 Cobra, OV-1C Mohawk and U-8 Seminole.

In order to fully appreciate the work of AMARC, one has only to look at the figures. Approximately 2,500 aircraft with an acquisition cost of almost seven billion dollars are in storage on 2,262 acres of desert, surrounded by thirteen miles of fencing. The latest available figures, for Fiscal Year 88, show that AMARC reclaimed 91,669 spare parts during the year. A total of 316 aircraft were received for storage, and 119 were withdrawn and returned to service.

The bottom line for the US taxpayer is that the value of the parts and aerospace vehicles placed back into service during FY 88 amounted to 247.7 million dollars. Considering that it cost 18.7 million dollars to operate the centre, it represents a return of thirteen dollars for every dollar spent, and that is good business.

Overleaf: Still wearing the badge and shark's mouth of the 35th Tactical Fighter Wing, Republic F-105G Thunderchief 62-4427 has been moved from AMARC to the nearby Pima Air Museum.

Opposite: Grumman C-1A Trader 136780 'Blue Ghost' has had its undercarriage and tail section removed since its arrival in 1978.

Below: Martin RB-57F Canberra NASA 925 was stored at AMARC barely long enough to acquire the inventory code BM141 before going 'over the road' to the Pima Air Museum.

Bottom: The 'Green Mountain Boys' of the Vermont Air National Guard retired Martin B-57C Canberra 53-3856 in December 1981.

Opposite: Rare white and red De Havilland Canada YC-7A
Caribou 57-3081 was severely damaged in a storm a few years
ago and is now fit only for scrap.

Below: Stored for the Air Force Museum, this North American
PA-48E is one of two prototypes.

Opposite: The first Grumman C-2A Greyhound to arrive at AMARC, 152790 is on display in Celebrity Row.

Bottom left: Boeing YC-14A 72-1874 was one of two produced as contenders for the Air Force Advanced Medium STOL transport competition, to find a replacement for the C-130 Hercules. The other YC-14A is on loan to the Pima Air Museum.

Below left: Still wearing the star and bar of the South Vietnamese Air Force, Douglas C-47D Skytrain 43-48859 has been in storage since August 1968.

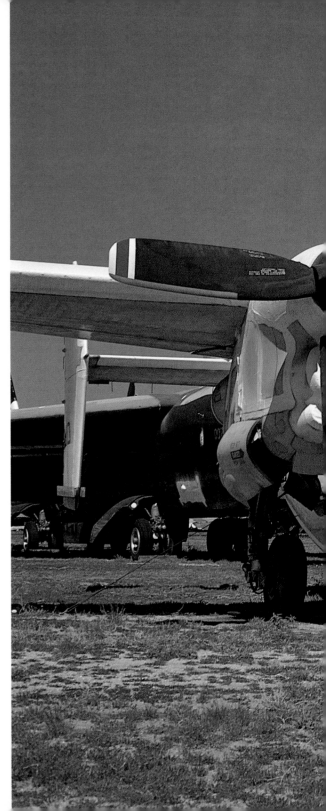

Overleaf: The last Lockheed C-121 Constellation at AMARC, EC-121S 54-0157, is stored on behalf of the Air Force Museum.

Opposite: Fairchild C-119L Flying Boxcar 53-8126 was retired by the 143rd Special Operations Squadron, Rhode Island Air National Guard in June 1975.

Below: A relic from the past. Boeing KC-97L Stratotanker 52-2656 was one of the last of the hundreds of C-97s to be sold at AMARC and now awaits its fate in a local scrapyard. *(Bob Greby)*

Overleaf: Over forty Lockheed C-130 Hercules transports are now in storage, from the early C-130 A models to the ski-equipped D models.

Opposite: One of a handful of Douglas C-124C Globemaster transports to escape the demise of the fleet at AMARC in the early 1970s, 52-1004 has been with the Pima Air Museum for fifteen years.

Below: The only Navy Lockheed DC-130A Hercules currently at AMARC is 158228, which served with Navy Composite Squadron VC-3 until retirement in 1979.

Opposite: Two exhibits on Celebrity Row: Fairchild UC-123K
Provider 55-4547 and Navy Convair C-131F 140999.

Below: This unusual nose belongs to Lockheed DC-130A
Hercules 56-0527, a Drone Director aircraft which arrived in
1986.

Opposite: Lockheed HC-130B Hercules 61-2083 being dismantled in March 1988 for shipment to Lockheed in California for use as a platform for a new AC-130 gunship.

Below: Having suffered extensive spare parts reclamation, this Lockheed HC-130B Hercules has now been transferred from the Coast Guard to the Air Force.

Opposite: The 'Happy Hooligans' of the North Dakota Air National Guard retired Convair C-131D Samaritan 54-2819 in 1987.

Below: The Air National Guard of Montana, the 'Big Sky Country', sent their Convair C-131D Samaritan 54-2823 to AMARC in January 1987.

Opposite: Purchased by Bob Hoover, the owner of Bob's Airpark, these former Trans World Airlines Boeing 707s will be dismantled and scrapped. Their military designation on the AMARC inventory is C-137B.

Below: The oldest-built Air Force Lockheed C-130A Hercules at AMARC, 53-3133, was operated by the ASD division of Air Force Systems Command until 1976.

Overleaf: Grumman E-2B Hawkeye 151724, on the wash rack in March 1988, is one of nineteen of the type in storage.

Opposite: One of the four Lockheed C-140B Jetstars to arrive in 1987, 61-2490 is on display in Celebrity Row.

Bottom left: As a condition of the SALT agreement, surplus Boeing B-52 Stratofortress bombers must be cut up and left for Soviet satellites to photograph before final disposal.
*(Graham Robson)*

Below left: Eight Grumman E-2B Hawkeye AEW aircraft are stored in the RIT area, including 149819 which arrived in 1983.

Opposite: The skull and lightning flash on the vertical stabilizer of this McDonnell Douglas F-4N Phantom II, identifies its previous unit as Marine Fighter Attack Squadron VMFA-531.

Below: Over 200 Navy and Marine McDonnell Douglas F-4 Phantoms are in storage, including F-4S 155863 which arrived in January 1988 after service with Marine Fighter Attack Squadron VMFA-235.

Opposite: The only black McDonnell Douglas F-4S Phantom II at AMARC, 155539 last served with Navy Air Test and Evaluation Squadron VX-4.

Below: The badge of the Navy Pacific Missile Test Centre adorns the tail of McDonnell Douglas DF-4J Phantom II 153084.

Opposite: Used as a spare parts aircraft since its arrival in 1977, McDonnell Douglas F-4N Phantom 151400 will eventually be sold for scrap.

Bottom left: Five years in the desert sun have faded the tail markings of Navy McDonnell Douglas F-4N Phantom II 151446, which once served with Fighter Squadron VF-154.

Below left: Five years of storage have done little to fade the tail markings of McDonnell Douglas F-4N Phantom II 153914 which last served with Navy Fighter Squadron VF-21.

Opposite: Splendidly restored by enthusiasts at the Pima Air Museum, Vought DF-8F Crusader 144427 once served with Navy Composite Squadron VC-7, but now wears the markings of Fighter Squadron VF-32. *(Bob Greby)*

Below: A red star signifying a MIG-kill marks Phantom 63-7589 as something special. Retired by the Texas Air National Guard in January 1987, this F-4C is worthy of preservation.

Opposite: The only midnight blue aircraft at AMARC, Douglas
F-10B Skynight 124610 arrived in August 1968 and has since
been transferred from the Navy to the Army.

Below: This Republic F-84F Thunderstreak comprises the front
of 51-1725 and the rear of 52-6563 and is stored on behalf of the
Air Force Museum.

Opposite: The tail section of North American F-100D Super Sabre 56-3081 is removed for overhaul and return to service after ten years in storage. Convair F-106A Delta Dart 57-2493 has just arrived.

Bottom left: The last of over 400 Grumman F-9 Cougars to be processed through AMARC, TF-9J 147283 arrived in May 1972 and is now on show in Celebrity Row.

Below left: Parked intact on Celebrity Row, Republic F-84F Thunderstreak 52-6701 arrived in 1971 and is one of three still at AMARC.

Opposite: The 123rd Fighter Interceptor Squadron of the
Oregon Air National Guard retired McDonnell Douglas F-4C
Phantom II 64-0811 in the summer of 1987.

Below: North American F-86H Sabre 53-1525 served with the
New Jersey Air National Guard before its retirement in the late
'60s. It has been splendidly restored by the Pima Air Museum.

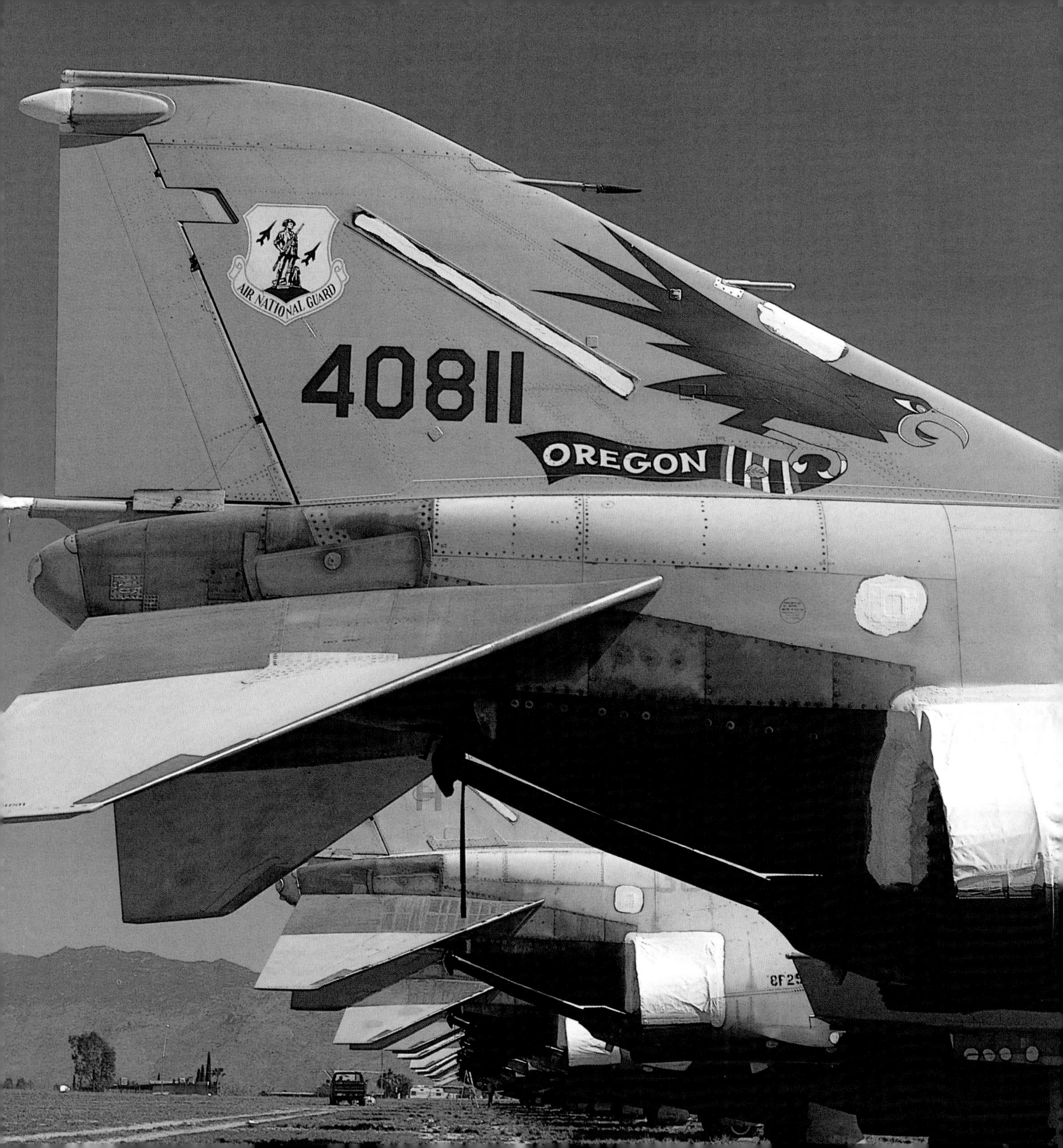
AIR NATIONAL GUARD
40811
OREGON

Opposite: Ten years after retirement by the Indiana Air
National Guard, North American F-100D Super Sabre 56-3195
prepares for return to service as a radio-controlled target drone.

Bottom left: The accessibility of the North American F-100
Super Sabre's engine is shown here as F-100D 55-3521 is split in
half. The red markings denote its role as a drone.

Below left: A relic from the good old days. The badge of the
363rd Tactical Reconnaissance Wing adorns this derelict
McDonnell RF-101B Voodoo in a scrapyard near AMARC.

Overleaf: Now resting in Celebrity Row, Convair F-102A Delta
Dagger 56-1266 was retired by the Connecticut Air National
Guard in June 1971.

Opposite: North American F-100 Super Sabres continue to
depart AMARC for conversion to radio-controlled drones,
and those remaining number just under 100.

Below: Less than a score of McDonnell F-101 Voodoos still
survive at AMARC. F-101B 58-0310 was retired by the
Minnesota Air National Guard in 1975.

Opposite: Work begins early in the morning on the first stages of preservation of Convair F-106B Delta Dart 57-2524, which now wears the AMARC inventory code number FN176.

Bottom left: Retired to AMARC late in 1984, Convair F-106A Delta Dart 56-0463 wears the colourful markings of the 87th Fighter Interceptor Squadron.

Below left: Parked on the arrival ramp, two-seater Convair F-106B Delta Dart 57-2517 was recently retired by the Massachusetts Air National Guard.

Overleaf: Two derelict P-3 Orions flank one of the last two Lockheed F-104D Starfighters still at AMARC. 57-1320 was retired by the Puerto Rico Air National Guard in 1975.

Opposite: Picked clean of all useful parts, Republic F-105 Thunderchief 63-8305 was a Wild Weasel with the 35th Tactical Fighter Wing until 1980.

Below: Less than two dozen Republic F-105 Thunderchiefs survive at AMARC. F-105D 59-1822 is held for the Air Force Museum.

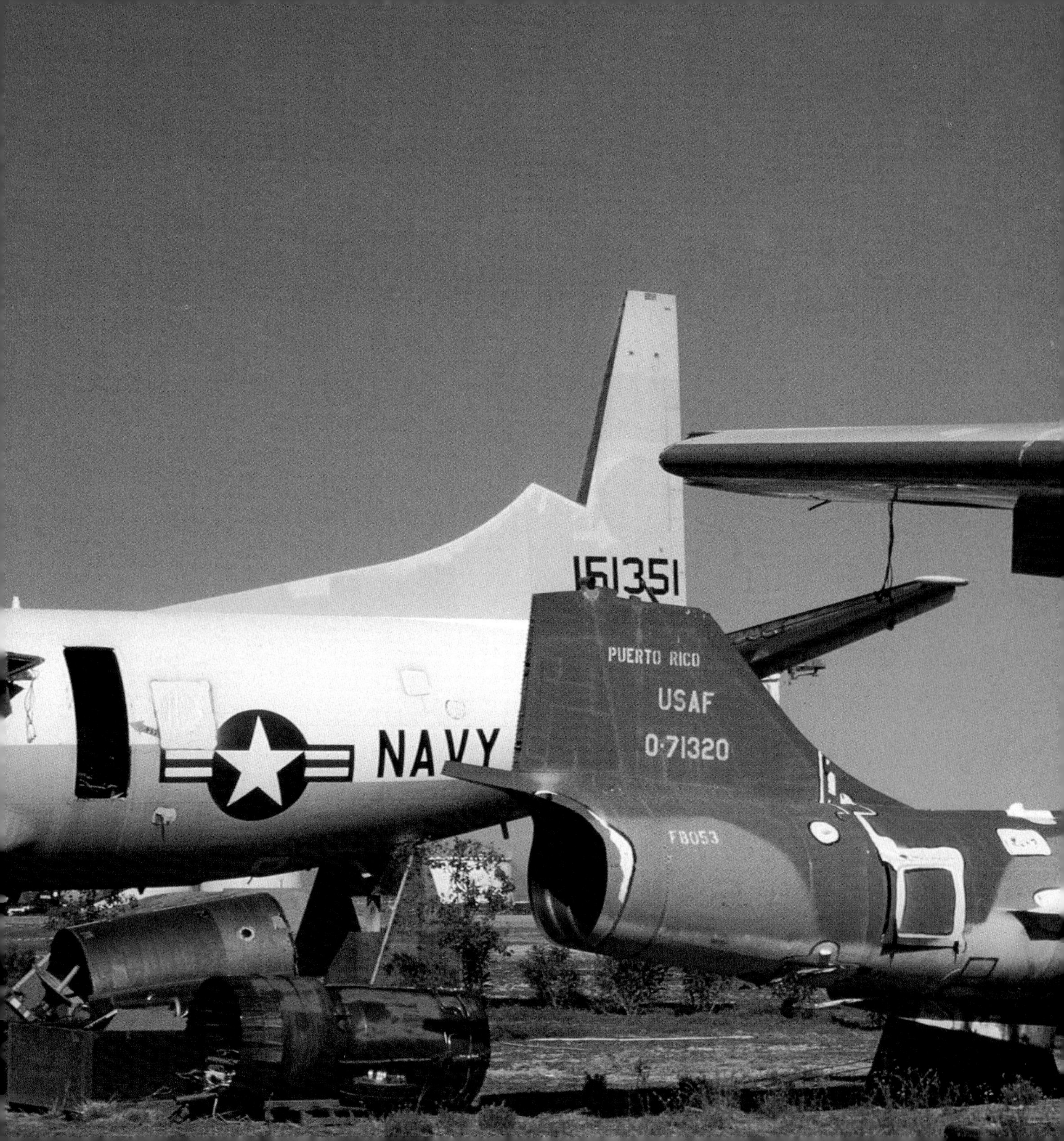
161351
NAVY
PUERTO RICO
USAF
0-71320
FB053

Opposite: The Tactical Air Command badge and markings of the 49th Fighter Interceptor Squadron adorn the vertical stabilizer of Convair F-106A Delta Dart 59-0093 which arrived in 1985.

Below: This line of Convair F-106 Delta Darts is only a small part of the 180 currently in storage.

Opposite: Eighteen years of spare parts reclamation has left
General Dynamics F-111A 65-5705 well and truly gutted.

Below: The odd-man out in this line of Convair F-106 Delta
Darts wears a tailor-made bag as a part of the desert storage test
programme.

Opposite: A most unusual aircraft. This Bell AH-1J Sea Cobra
wears the camouflage and serial number 3-4412 of the Iranian
Army and has been in storage since June 1980.

Below: As Bell TH-1F Iroquois 66-1231 clearly shows,
helicopters require more preservation effort than most
fixed-wing aircraft.

Overleaf: As two Fairchild Republic A-10A Thunderbolt II aircraft approach in the distance, these Piasecki CH-21B Workhorse helicopters sit forlornly in the Allied Aircraft storage yard, with 53-4389 nearest the camera. *(Bob Greby)*

Opposite: Newly arrived Marines Bell AH-1J Sea Cobra 157799 has been allocated the AMARC inventory code number 7H177.

Bottom left: Sikorsky CH-53A Sea Stallion 152411 is one of fifteen that the Marines retired to AMARC in 1987.

Below left: The only Boeing (Vertol) Sea Knight currently at AMARC, rare NCH-46D 153374 has been a resident since 1971.

Opposite: Now finally withdrawn as a primary training helicopter by the Army, these Hughes TH-55A Osage two-seaters will probably end up on the civil market.

Bottom left: An early test aircraft, Navy Sikorsky SH-60B Sea Hawk 161172 has been in storage since February 1984 and will soon return to service.

Below left: Wearing the easily identifiable markings of the Coast Guard, Sikorsky HH-52A Seaguard 1422 is one of over thirty to arrive since 1986.

Opposite: With its engine access cover wide open, this Sikorsky H-34 Choctaw lies derelict at Bob's Airpark.

Below: Wearing rather unusual markings and serial number, this Sikorsky H-34 Choctaw sits in the sun at Bob's Airpark, not far from AMARC.

Opposite: Twenty-six Army Vertol CH-47A Chinook twin-rotor helicopters are in storage. 62-2131 arrived in November 1975 and wears the AMARC inventory code XM006.

Below: Well preserved and on display in Celebrity Row, Coast Guard Aerospatiale HH-65A Dauphin 6509 is the only one of its kind at AMARC.

Opposite: Twelve of the thirteen Navy Lockheed P-2H
Neptunes still at AMARC are held for the Naval Aviation
Museum.

Below: Over 160 Cessna 0-2 Super Skymaster observation
aircraft are in storage, including 68-11050, which was previously
flown by the Michigan Air National Guard.

Overleaf: Since its arrival in 1984, Lockheed P-3A Orion 151361 has been company for these former Air Force C-130s.

Opposite: A large number of Lockheed SP-2 Neptunes have been sold over the last couple of years. Some still reside at Bob's Airpark, just outside AMARC.

Bottom left: Purchased in a surplus aircraft sale, these Grumman S-2 Trackers are stored by Consolidated Aeronautics not far from AMARC. IS389 nearest the camera is US-2D 148750.

Below left: Still wearing the badge of Navy Patrol Squadron VP-94, Lockheed SP-2H Neptune 147950 has been in storage since July 1976.

Opposite: Parked in its shipboard pose with folded wings, Grumman US-2B Tracker 136643 served at Alameda Naval Air Station until December 1978.

Bottom left: Only fifty Grumman S-2 Trackers remain at AMARC, including US-2B 136719 which arrived in April 1981.

Below left: Item number 61 in surplus aircraft sale 41-1100, this Grumman S-2 Tracker shows the extensive reclamation that the type underwent prior to sale.

Opposite: Currently stored in Bob's Airpark, Convair VT-29B 51-7900 was sold to Desert Air Parts in 1977 and wears the AMARC inventory code TB269.

Bottom left: Bereft of its power plant, North American T-28B Trojan 138339 is stored on behalf of the Navy Aviation Museum.

Below left: Retired by Navy Anti-Submarine Warfare Squadron VS-33 in 1975, Grumman S-2G Tracker 152810 is now used as a resting place for weary birds.

Opposite: Grumman C-1A Trader 146052 is earmarked for the
Navy Aviation Museum, together with the rare Lockheed
EP-2H Neptune 148338 in the background.

Below: Now picked clean of almost every usable spare part,
Convair C-131D 54-2805 arrived at AMARC on 9 January 1975
from the Texas Air National Guard.

Opposite: A new arrival in February 1988, Lockheed T-33A
Shooting Star 58-0506 joins 160 other Air Force T-33s in
storage.

Bottom left: This line of North American T-39 Sabreliners
contrasts with the colourful row of F-106s in the background.
Over one hundred T-39s are in storage, including CT-39A
62-4457 nearest the camera.

Below: One of the very latest Phantoms to arrive at AMARC.
This Marine F-4S wears the serial number 155805 and the
markings of Marine Fighter Attack Squadron VMFA-212
'Lancers'. *(Bob Shane)*

Opposite: Like ducks out of water: stored at Bob's Airpark for
the Grumman Corporation, HU-16E Albatross 7227 once
served with the Coast Guard, and HU-16C 141262 behind
served with the Navy.

Below: Still intact and a possible candidate for restoration,
Grumman HU-16E Albatross 7245 ended its career with the
Coast Guard at Cape Cod. *(Bob Greby)*

Opposite: Retired by Navy Training Wing TW-5 in 1978, these North American T-28C Trojans lie in the sun at Bob's Airpark.

Below left: Two Fairchild Republic T-46A trainers are currently at AMARC. 85-1596 is on display on Celebrity Row wearing the inventory code TM001.

Bottom left: Now a wreck in the RIT area, Lockheed T-33A Shooting Star 58-2098 was used by Aerospace Defense Command until 1975.

Opposite: One of the many Beechcraft U-8 Seminole utility aircraft sold to the public over the last couple of years, U-8D 57-6041 is stored at Bob's Airpark, still wearing the sale number 16.

Below: One of the older Grumman OV-1B Mohawks at AMARC, 62-5892 arrived in August 1972, and this shot illustrates the unusual design of the type.

Overleaf: This aerial view of AMARC shows B-52
Stratofortress and B-57 Canberra bombers, C-130 Hercules
transports, Navy S-2 Trackers, Marine AV-8s, Army OV-1
Mohawks, Air Force F-4 Phantoms and a sprinkling of Navy
P-3 Orions. *(Graham Robson)*

Opposite: One of a handful of two-seater AV-8s at AMARC,
TAV-8A 159383 arrived late in 1987 from Marine Attack
Training Squadron VMAT-203.

Below: This line of vertical take-off Marine Harriers ends with
the long noses of the only five TAV-8 trainers to arrive to date.

Opposite: The squadron badge of Navy Logistic Support
Squadron VR-46, worn by Douglas C-118B Liftmaster 131597
which was retired by the unit in February 1985.

Below: The red markings and Aerospace Defense Command
badge belong to Martin EB-57E Canberra 55-4240 which was
retired by the 17th Defense Systems Evaluation Squadron in
July 1979.

597 *na*

VR-46

8C0

Opposite: Bell UH-1H 63-8836, wearing the AMARC
inventory code XA345, arrived in October 1988 and heads the
line of some of the 2,300 Hueys to be retired by the Army over
the next two decades. *(Bob Shane)*

Below: The squadron badge of Navy Tactical Electronic
Warfare Squadron VAQ-208, painted just above the refuelling
probe of Douglas KA-3B Skywarrior 138965 which arrived in
July 1975.

Opposite: The rather stark markings on this McDonnell Douglas F-4S Phantom II identify it as 153900, formerly NF-212 with Navy Fighter Squadron VF-151.

Bottom left: This long line of Convair F-106 Delta Darts wear the yellow and black markings of the 86th Fighter Interceptor Squadron and the maroon of the 87th Fighter Interceptor Squadron.

Below left: Only the bare bones remain of these four General Dynamics F-111As, in storage since 1971 and currently stored in the RIT area.

Opposite: The colourful markings of the 136th Fighter
Interceptor Squadron adorn McDonnell Douglas F-4C Phantom
II 64-0836. This Air National Guard unit is based at Niagara
Falls Airport in New York State.

Below: An extremely unsightly, but cost effective method of
protecting aircraft in storage, these plastic covers were to have
replaced the traditional Spraylat preservative, but the project is
now believed to be cancelled.

Opposite: Formerly used by the Oregon Air National Guard,
McDonnell Douglas F-4C Phantom II 64-0888 arrived at
AMARC in October 1986.

Bottom left: The badge of Navy Helicopter Combat Support
Squadron HC-6 on a Boeing Vertol UH-46A Sea Knight which
has since been sold for scrap.

Below left: The AMARC inventory code FN073 identifies this
aircraft as Convair F-106A Delta Dart 59-0093. Profusely
stencilled and wearing the badge of the 86th Fighter Interceptor
Squadron, it arrived in 1985.

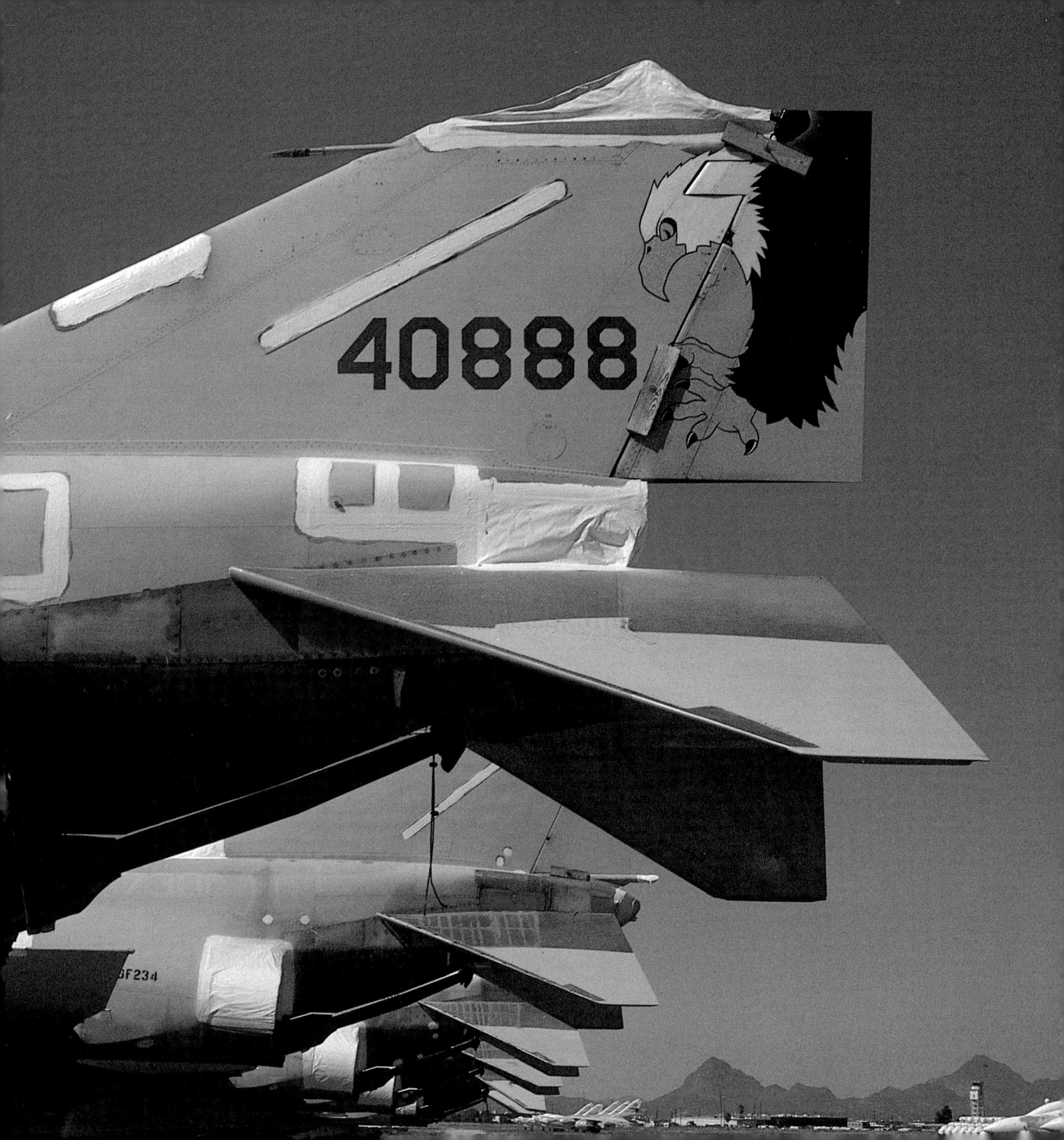
40888
BF234

Overleaf: Helicopter tail booms from (left to right) Air Force TH-IF 66-1235, Navy UH-1E 151271 and Iranian Army AH-1J 3-4412.

Opposite: Camouflaged McDonnell Douglas F-4C Phantom II 63-7704 from the Oregon Air National Guard, with Navy Vought RF-8G Crusader 144618 behind.

Below: Photographed on the arrival ramp in March 1988, Convair F-106 Delta Darts from the 101st Fighter Interceptor Squadron Massachusetts and 186th FIS Montana, Air National Guard Units.

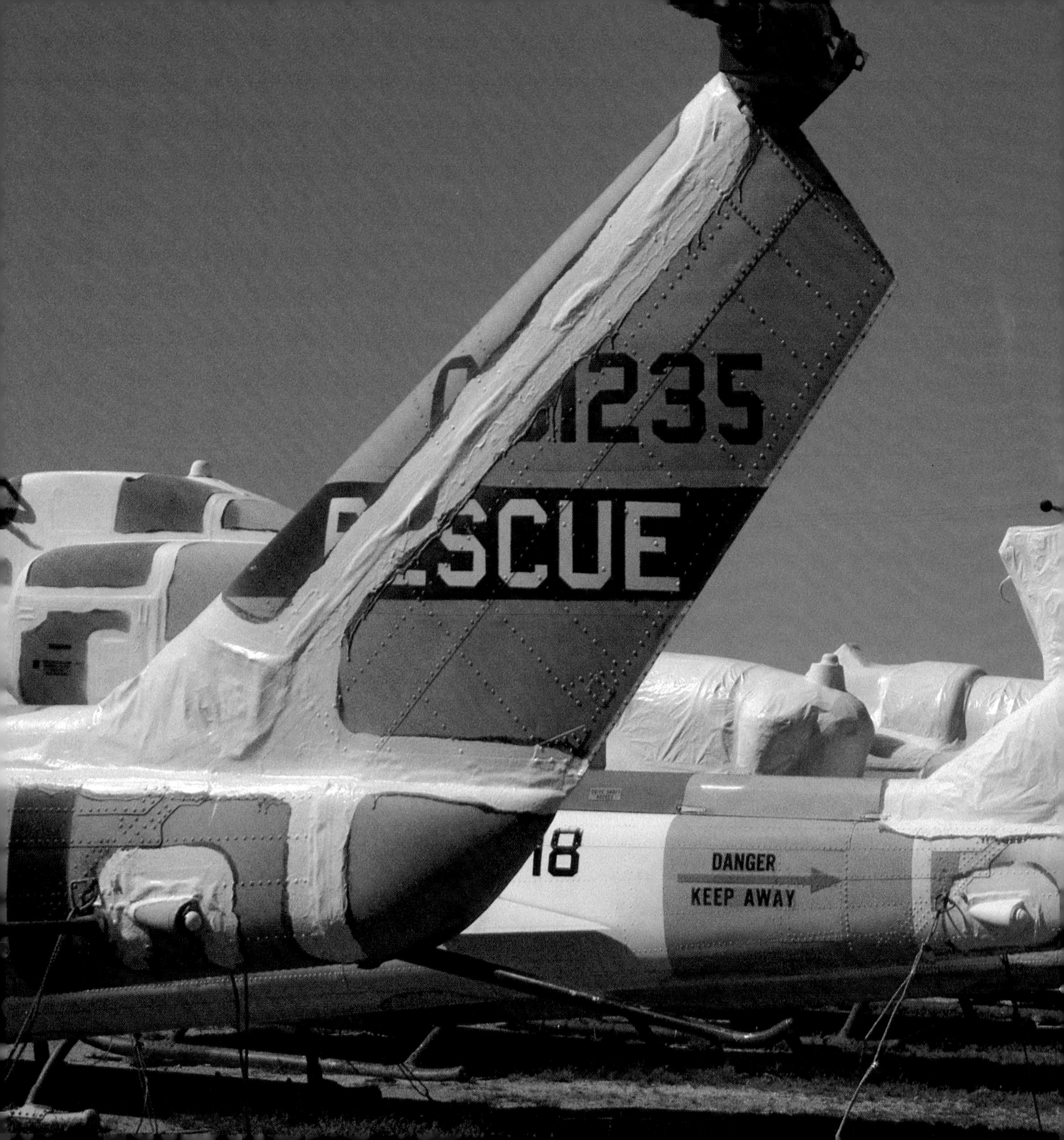
1235
ESCUE
18
DANGER
KEEP AWAY

Opposite: The oldest-built Boeing B-52C Stratofortress in AMARC, 53-0400 sits in the DROP AREA awaiting disposal.

Below: Flown by the 109th Tactical Airlift Group of the New York Air National Guard, these ski-equipped Lockheed C-130D Hercules transports were used to resupply Distant Early Warning (DEW) radar sites north of the Arctic Circle until their replacement in 1985 by LC-130Hs. *(Bob Greby)*

Opposite: Grumman E-2B Hawkeye 149819 arrived early in
1983 and is now in the RIT area, still wearing the markings of
Navy Airborne Early Warning Squadron CARAEWRON 88.

Below: The last five Fairchild C-119L Flying Boxcars at
AMARC were used by Air National Guard Special Operations
Squadrons and retired in 1975.

Overleaf: Now replaced by McDonnell Douglas F-4S Phantom IIs, these F-4Js still wear the markings of Marine Fighter Attack Squadron VMFA-112.

Opposite and below left: The rampaging hog badge of the 184th Tactical Fighter Squadron, Arkansas Air National Guard, adorns McDonnell Douglas F-4C Phantom II 64-0726.

Bottom left: Being prepared for departure in March 1988, Grumman A-6E Intruder 152935 has been in storage since 1980.

Overleaf: Boeing B-52D Stratofortresses 55-0091 and 56-0596 arrived in 1982 and are part of Strategic Air Command's war reserve.

Opposite: One of two Sikorsky CH-3E at AMARC, 65-12788 on Celebrity Row once served with the 432nd Tactical Drone Group at Davis-Monthan Air Force Base.

Below: The tailbooms of the twenty-nine Bell TH-57A Sea Rangers in storage during the author's visit. 157355 nearest the camera was the first to arrive in December 1985.

Opposite: Painted high visibility red and used by Boeing and the Air Force Flight Dynamics Laboratory for Control Configured Vehicle tests, Boeing NB-52E Stratofortress 56-0632 arrived for storage in June 1974.

Below left: The end of the line for some of the Convair C-131 Samaritans at AMARC. 51-5127, the C-131A nearest the camera, arrived in 1977.

Bottom left: Many of the fifty Convair C-131 Samaritan transport aircraft are preserved for possible sale. Rows of Phantoms can be seen in the background.

Opposite: Bell UH-1H 64-13827 displays the rare nose art
CHRISTINE, painted by 'PFC McCarthy', alongside the
AMARC inventory code XA336. *(Bob Shane)*

Below: Bell OH-58A Kiowa light observation helicopters are
also now arriving for storage, as the Army begins its plan to
withdraw from service 1,350 aircraft before 1992. *(Bob Shane)*

# Tour Information

At the present time, tours of the centre are being conducted on a reservation basis only. On Monday and Wednesday mornings the tour is relatively short and includes a drive down the Davis-Monthan flight line and around the storage areas. Visitors on this tour are not allowed to leave the bus. For enthusiasts and photographers a four-hour photographic tour takes place at 08:00 on the second Saturday of each month and people are allowed off the tour bus to photograph aircraft. For further information contact the Public Affairs Office, 836th Air Division, Davis-Monthan AFB, Arizona 85707, USA. Telephone (602) 748-3358.

# Aircraft Type

| | *Quantity* |
|---|---|
| A-3 Skywarrior (Douglas) | 33 |
| A-4 Skyhawk (Douglas) | 33 |
| A-6 Intruder (Grumman) | 1 |
| A-7 Corsair II (LTV) | 165 |
| 0A-37 Dragonfly (Cessna) | 4 |
| PA-48E Enforcer (Piper) | 1 |
| B-47 Stratojet (Boeing) | 2 |
| B-52 Stratofortress (Boeing) | 228 |
| B-57 Canberra (Martin) | 35 |
| C-1 Trader (Grumman) | 31 |
| C-2 Greyhound (Grumman) | 6 |
| C-7 Caribou (DHC) | 2 |
| YC-14 (Boeing) | 2 |
| YC-15 (McDD) | 2 |
| C-47 Skytrain (Douglas) | 3 |
| C-118 Liftmaster (Douglas) | 12 |
| C-119 Flying Boxcar (Fairchild) | 5 |
| C-121 Constellation (Lockheed) | 1 |
| C-123 Provider (Fairchild) | 32 |
| C-130 Hercules (Lockheed) | 42 |
| C-131 Samaritan (Convair) | 52 |
| C-135 Stratotanker (Boeing) | 2 |
| C-137 (Boeing 707) | 146 |
| VC-140 Jetstar (Lockheed) | 6 |
| E-2 Hawkeye (Grumman) | 19 |
| F-4 Phantom (McDD) | 380 |
| F-8 Crusader (LTV) | 46 |
| F-9 Cougar (Grumman) | 1 |
| EF-10 Skynight (Douglas) | 5 |
| F-11 Tiger (Grumman) | 1 |
| F-84 Thunderflash (Republic) | 3 |
| F-100 Super Sabre (NAA) | 95 |
| F-101 Voodoo (McD) | 15 |
| F-102 Delta Dagger (Convair) | 8 |
| F-104 Starfighter (Lockheed) | 2 |
| F-105 Thunderchief (Republic) | 18 |
| F-106 Delta Dart (Convair) | 184 |
| F-111 (General Dynamics) | 8 |
| AH-1 Cobra (Bell) | 11 |
| UH-1 Iroquois (Bell) | 106 |
| H-3 Sea King (Sikorsky) | 2 |
| H-34 Choctaw/Seabat (Sikorsky) | 6 |
| H-46 Sea Knight (Vertol) | 1 |
| H-47 Chinook (Vertol) | 26 |
| HH-52 Seaguard (Sikorksy) | 36 |
| CH-53 Sea Stallion (Sikorsky) | 15 |
| TH-55 Osage (Hughes) | 78 |
| TH-57 Sea Ranger (Bell) | 29 |
| OH-58 Kiowa (Bell) | 35 |
| O-2 Skymaster (Cessna) | 163 |
| SP-2 Neptune (Lockheed) | 20 |
| P-3 Orion (Lockheed) | 27 |
| S-2 Tracker (Grumman) | 51 |
| T-1 Seastar (Lockheed) | 1 |
| T-28 Trojan (NAA) | 48 |
| T-29 (Convair) | 5 |
| T-33 (Lockheed) | 184 |
| T-34 Mentor (Beech) | 19 |
| T-38 Talon (Northrop) | 13 |
| T-39 Sabreliner (NAA) | 117 |
| T-46 (Fairchild Republic) | 2 |
| U-8 Seminole (Beech) | 7 |
| HU-16 Albatross (Grumman) | 4 |
| OV-1 Mohawk (Grumman) | 46 |
| AV-8 Harrier (HSA) | 42 |

Total of 2725. Comprising 1574 Air Force, 865 Navy, 248 Army and 38 Coast Guard.